Meet Karen

As an entrepreneur, business owner, mother of three, I often felt the weight of financial burden on my shoulders.

Since my teen years I had always been pretty responsible with money and other areas in my life. I was under the impression that working hard and having delayed gratification would pay off sooner or later. Although it did in some ways, I realized that there was a huge gap between where I was financially verses where I expected to be. It wasn't until I started praying the right prayers and appling all of the right principles that I realized there was a method to the madness.

I began to format a monthly budget sheet along with a debt free planner board to easily track expenses, apply the proper budget, and eliminate debt.

I became a better stewart over my finances, while at the same time, getting an understanding of God's plan for my life. My desire is to help others ditch living paycheck to paycheck and apply some of the same principles that it took me years to grasp.

I want to Congratulate you!!! By purchasing this journal you are one step closer to financial freedom and living life from a different view.

Tips

While moving through this journal I suggest that you take time to do the following

• If married work on your budget and savings with your spouse if possible.

• Pay with debit/check(for easy tracking)

• Do not add to your debt (pay directly)

• Keep receipts each day for logging.

• Set a time daily or weekly to record proper records.

• Sell/downgrade everything you don't absolutely need at this time (this is an option to reach your goals quickly)

• When you cut costs as well as earn extra money be sure to separate that amount into a different account.(for example I cut the cable bill to $50 less a month I will put $50 each month in another account for savings or for paying down debt snowball)

I've experienced the best results while tithing and building a closer relationship with God. Congrats You've made the first step to living a more prosperous life!

My Financial Freedom Journey

> "For the Lord Your God will bless you as he has promised you will lend to many nations and not borrow"
>
> —DEUTERONOMY 28:12

Monthly View

MONTH & YEAR: _____

THIS MONTH'S GOALS

_____
_____
_____
_____

WEEKLY GOALS

_____
_____
_____
_____

DAILY GOALS

_____
_____
_____
_____

SUN	MON	TUE	WED	THU	FRI	SAT

Monthly Budget

HOME	
Mortgage/ Rent	$
Home Insurance	$
Maintenance	$
TOTAL	

CHILDREN	
Child Care	$
Sports	$
	$
TOTAL	

UTILITIES	
Electricity	$
Water/ Sewer	$
Garbage	$
Home Phone	$
Cell Phone	$
TV/ Internet	$
TOTAL	

TRANSPORTATION	
Car Payment	$
Insurance	$
Maintenance	$
Fuel	$
	$
	$
TOTAL	

PERSONAL	
Gym	$
Hair/ Grooming	$
Clothes/ Shoes	$
Vacation	$
Veterinarian	$
TOTAL	

LOANS/DEBT	
Student	$
Personal	$
Credit Cards	$
	$
	$
TOTAL	

MEDICAL	
Doctor	$
Dentist	$
Pharmacy	$
TOTAL	

OTHER	
	$
	$
	$
	$
	$
	$
	$
	$
	$
	$
TOTAL	

INCOME	
Date:	$
Date:	$
Date:	$
Date:	$
TOTAL	

TOTAL INCOME		TOTAL EXPENSES		DIFFERENCE	

Expense Tracker

DATE	DESCRIPTION	CATEGORY	AMOUNT
		TOTAL EXPENSE	

Expense Tracker

DATE	DESCRIPTION	CATEGORY	AMOUNT
		TOTAL EXPENSE	

Expense Tracker

DATE	DESCRIPTION	CATEGORY	AMOUNT
		TOTAL EXPENSE	

Expense Tracker

DATE	DESCRIPTION	CATEGORY	AMOUNT
		TOTAL EXPENSE	

Expense Tracker

DATE	DESCRIPTION	CATEGORY	AMOUNT
		TOTAL EXPENSE	

Savings Summary

DATE	EMERGENCY FUND	SAVINGS	INVESTMENT

TOTAL SAVINGS

Debt Snowball

List debts smallest to largest. Pay down the smallest debt while paying the minimum payment on all the other debt.

NAME DEBT.	TOTAL BALANCE	MINIMUM PAYMENT	SNOWBALL PAYMENT
TOTAL			

Total Balance - Total Payment = New Balance

Pay off Goals

Amount of months set to pay off smallest debt = _____

Surplus needed each month to reach this goal(smallest debt ÷ number of months) = _____

(Interest not included in calculation)

Goal Planner

The broken down monthly and weekly steps to help you reach your end of the year goals.

This years Goal is

What steps will I take each month to reach this year's goals

What steps will I take each week to reach my monthly goals

My prayer is

Scripture reading

God My Provider

> "And God will supply every one of your needs according to his riches in glory"
>
> -PHILIPPIANS 4:19

Monthly View

MONTH & YEAR: _____

THIS MONTH'S GOALS

_____
_____
_____
_____
_____

WEEKLY GOALS

_____
_____
_____
_____
_____

DAILY GOALS

_____
_____
_____
_____
_____

SUN	MON	TUE	WED	THU	FRI	SAT

Monthly Budget

HOME	
Mortgage/ Rent	$
Home Insurance	$
Maintenance	$
TOTAL	

CHILDREN	
Child Care	$
Sports	$
	$
TOTAL	

UTILITIES	
Electricity	$
Water/ Sewer	$
Garbage	$
Home Phone	$
Cell Phone	$
TV/ Internet	$
TOTAL	

TRANSPORTATION	
Car Payment	$
Insurance	$
Maintenance	$
Fuel	$
	$
	$
TOTAL	

PERSONAL	
Gym	$
Hair/ Grooming	$
Clothes/ Shoes	$
Vacation	$
Veterinarian	$
TOTAL	

LOANS/DEBT	
Student	$
Personal	$
Credit Cards	$
	$
	$
TOTAL	

MEDICAL	
Doctor	$
Dentist	$
Pharmacy	$
TOTAL	

OTHER	
	$
	$
	$
	$
	$
	$
	$
	$
	$
	$
TOTAL	

INCOME	
Date:	$
Date:	$
Date:	$
Date:	$
TOTAL	

TOTAL INCOME		TOTAL EXPENSES		DIFFERENCE	

Expense Tracker

DATE	DESCRIPTION	CATEGORY	AMOUNT
		TOTAL EXPENSE	

Expense Tracker

DATE	DESCRIPTION	CATEGORY	AMOUNT

| | TOTAL EXPENSE | |

Expense Tracker

DATE	DESCRIPTION	CATEGORY	AMOUNT
		TOTAL EXPENSE	

Expense Tracker

DATE	DESCRIPTION	CATEGORY	AMOUNT
		TOTAL EXPENSE	

Expense Tracker

DATE	DESCRIPTION	CATEGORY	AMOUNT

TOTAL EXPENSE

Savings Summary

DATE	EMERGENCY FUND	SAVINGS	INVESTMENT

TOTAL SAVINGS

Debt Snowball

List debts smallest to largest. Pay down the smallest debt while paying the minimum payment on all the other debt.

NAME DEBT.	TOTAL BALANCE	MINIMUM PAYMENT	SNOWBALL PAYMENT
TOTAL			

Total Balance - Total Payment = New Balance

Pay off Goals

Amount of months set to pay off smallest debt = _____

Surplus needed each month to reach this goal(smallest debt ÷ number of months) = _____
(Interest not included in calculation)

Have I paid down my debt snowball this month?

How will I stay on track?

My plan to make more money is

My prayer is

Scripture reading

My Obedience

> "And if you are untrustworthy with worldly wealth, who will trust you with the true riches in heaven"
>
> -LUKE 16:11

Monthly View

MONTH & YEAR: _____

THIS MONTH'S GOALS

_____
_____
_____
_____

WEEKLY GOALS

_____
_____
_____
_____

DAILY GOALS

_____
_____
_____
_____

SUN	MON	TUE	WED	THU	FRI	SAT

My Map To Financial Freedom

"Write the vision and make it plain." -Habakkuk 2:2

This map will be a visual reminder of where you are now and how you will get to where you are going.

Monthly Budget

HOME	
Mortgage/ Rent	$
Home Insurance	$
Maintenance	$
TOTAL	

CHILDREN	
Child Care	$
Sports	$
	$
TOTAL	

UTILITIES	
Electricity	$
Water/ Sewer	$
Garbage	$
Home Phone	$
Cell Phone	$
TV/ Internet	$
TOTAL	

TRANSPORTATION	
Car Payment	$
Insurance	$
Maintenance	$
Fuel	$
	$
	$
TOTAL	

PERSONAL	
Gym	$
Hair/ Grooming	$
Clothes/ Shoes	$
Vacation	$
Veterinarian	$
TOTAL	

LOANS/DEBT	
Student	$
Personal	$
Credit Cards	$
	$
	$
TOTAL	

MEDICAL	
Doctor	$
Dentist	$
Pharmacy	$
TOTAL	

OTHER	
	$
	$
	$
	$
	$
	$
	$
	$
	$
TOTAL	

INCOME	
Date:	$
Date:	$
Date:	$
Date:	$
TOTAL	

TOTAL INCOME		TOTAL EXPENSES		DIFFERENCE	

Expense Tracker

DATE	DESCRIPTION	CATEGORY	AMOUNT
		TOTAL EXPENSE	

Expense Tracker

DATE	DESCRIPTION	CATEGORY	AMOUNT

TOTAL EXPENSE	

Expense Tracker

DATE	DESCRIPTION	CATEGORY	AMOUNT
		TOTAL EXPENSE	

Expense Tracker

DATE	DESCRIPTION	CATEGORY	AMOUNT

TOTAL EXPENSE	

Expense Tracker

DATE	DESCRIPTION	CATEGORY	AMOUNT
		TOTAL EXPENSE	

Savings Summary

DATE	EMERGENCY FUND	SAVINGS	INVESTMENT

TOTAL SAVINGS	

Debt Snowball

List debts smallest to largest. Pay down the smallest debt while paying the minimum payment on all the other debt.

NAME DEBT.	TOTAL BALANCE	MINIMUM PAYMENT	SNOWBALL PAYMENT
TOTAL			

Total Balance - Total Payment = New Balance

Pay off Goals

Amount of months set to pay off smallest debt = ...

Surplus needed each month to reach this goal (smallest debt ÷ number of months) = ...
(Interest not included in calculation)

Have I been transferring my extra savings and/or my extra income into a different account away from bill or spending money?

___

Have I worked overtime or picked up a side job to add to savings and pay down my debt snowball? If so explain

___

Did I achieve last month's goals?

___

My prayer is

Scripture reading

Making Room

"Give and you shall receive. Your gift will return to you in full pressed down shaken together and running over, and pouring into your lap."

-LUKE 6:38

Monthly View

MONTH & YEAR: _____

THIS MONTH'S GOALS

_____
_____
_____
_____

WEEKLY GOALS

_____
_____
_____
_____

DAILY GOALS

_____
_____
_____
_____

SUN	MON	TUE	WED	THU	FRI	SAT

Monthly Budget

HOME	
Mortgage/ Rent	$
Home Insurance	$
Maintenance	$
TOTAL	

CHILDREN	
Child Care	$
Sports	$
	$
TOTAL	

UTILITIES	
Electricity	$
Water/ Sewer	$
Garbage	$
Home Phone	$
Cell Phone	$
TV/ Internet	$
TOTAL	

TRANSPORTATION	
Car Payment	$
Insurance	$
Maintenance	$
Fuel	$
	$
	$
TOTAL	

PERSONAL	
Gym	$
Hair/ Grooming	$
Clothes/ Shoes	$
Vacation	$
Veterinarian	$
TOTAL	

LOANS/DEBT	
Student	$
Personal	$
Credit Cards	$
	$
	$
TOTAL	

MEDICAL	
Doctor	$
Dentist	$
Pharmacy	$
TOTAL	

OTHER	
	$
	$
	$
	$
	$
	$
	$
	$
	$
	$
TOTAL	

INCOME	
Date:	$
Date:	$
Date:	$
Date:	$
TOTAL	

TOTAL INCOME		TOTAL EXPENSES		DIFFERENCE	

Expense Tracker

DATE	DESCRIPTION	CATEGORY	AMOUNT

| TOTAL EXPENSE | |

Expense Tracker

DATE	DESCRIPTION	CATEGORY	AMOUNT

| | TOTAL EXPENSE | |

Expense Tracker

DATE	DESCRIPTION	CATEGORY	AMOUNT
		TOTAL EXPENSE	

Expense Tracker

DATE	DESCRIPTION	CATEGORY	AMOUNT
		TOTAL EXPENSE	

Expense Tracker

DATE	DESCRIPTION	CATEGORY	AMOUNT

| | | TOTAL EXPENSE | |

Savings Summary

DATE	EMERGENCY FUND	SAVINGS	INVESTMENT

TOTAL SAVINGS

Debt Snowball

List debts smallest to largest. Pay down the smallest debt while paying the minimum payment on all the other debt.

NAME DEBT.	TOTAL BALANCE	MINIMUM PAYMENT	SNOWBALL PAYMENT
TOTAL			

Total Balance - Total Payment = New Balance

Pay off Goals

Amount of months set to pay off smallest debt = _____

Surplus needed each month to reach this goal (smallest debt ÷ number of months) = _____
(Interest not included in calculation)

I am a giver who

My money story is

My prayer is

Scripture reading

A New Thing

> "Remember not the former things nor consider the things of the old behold I am doing a new thing"
>
> -ISAIAH 43:18-19

Monthly View

MONTH & YEAR: _____

THIS MONTH'S GOALS

WEEKLY GOALS

DAILY GOALS

SUN	MON	TUE	WED	THU	FRI	SAT

Monthly Budget

HOME	
Mortgage/ Rent	$
Home Insurance	$
Maintenance	$
TOTAL	

CHILDREN	
Child Care	$
Sports	$
	$
TOTAL	

UTILITIES	
Electricity	$
Water/ Sewer	$
Garbage	$
Home Phone	$
Cell Phone	$
TV/ Internet	$
TOTAL	

TRANSPORTATION	
Car Payment	$
Insurance	$
Maintenance	$
Fuel	$
	$
	$
TOTAL	

PERSONAL	
Gym	$
Hair/ Grooming	$
Clothes/ Shoes	$
Vacation	$
Veterinarian	$
TOTAL	

LOANS/DEBT	
Student	$
Personal	$
Credit Cards	$
	$
	$
TOTAL	

MEDICAL	
Doctor	$
Dentist	$
Pharmacy	$
TOTAL	

OTHER	
	$
	$
	$
	$
	$
	$
	$
	$
	$
	$
TOTAL	

INCOME	
Date:	$
Date:	$
Date:	$
Date:	$
TOTAL	

TOTAL INCOME		TOTAL EXPENSES		DIFFERENCE	

Expense Tracker

DATE	DESCRIPTION	CATEGORY	AMOUNT
		TOTAL EXPENSE	

Expense Tracker

DATE	DESCRIPTION	CATEGORY	AMOUNT

TOTAL EXPENSE

Expense Tracker

DATE	DESCRIPTION	CATEGORY	AMOUNT

TOTAL EXPENSE	

Expense Tracker

DATE	DESCRIPTION	CATEGORY	AMOUNT
		TOTAL EXPENSE	

Expense Tracker

DATE	DESCRIPTION	CATEGORY	AMOUNT

TOTAL EXPENSE

Savings Summary

DATE	EMERGENCY FUND	SAVINGS	INVESTMENT

TOTAL SAVINGS

Debt Snowball

List debts smallest to largest. Pay down the smallest debt while paying the minimum payment on all the other debt.

NAME DEBT.	TOTAL BALANCE	MINIMUM PAYMENT	SNOWBALL PAYMENT
TOTAL			

Total Balance - Total Payment = New Balance

Pay off Goals

Amount of months set to pay off smallest debt = _____

Surplus needed each month to reach this goal (smallest debt ÷ number of months) = _____

(Interest not included in calculation)

Things that keep me motivated

What goals did I achieve last month

My struggle areas are

My prayer is

Scripture reading

Mindset Shift

> "To put off your old self which belongs to your former manner of life and is corrupt through deceitful desires and to be renewed in the mind"
>
> -EPHESIANS 4:22-24

Monthly View

MONTH & YEAR: _____

THIS MONTH'S GOALS

WEEKLY GOALS

DAILY GOALS

SUN	MON	TUE	WED	THU	FRI	SAT

Monthly Budget

HOME	
Mortgage/ Rent	$
Home Insurance	$
Maintenance	$
TOTAL	

CHILDREN	
Child Care	$
Sports	$
	$
TOTAL	

UTILITIES	
Electricity	$
Water/ Sewer	$
Garbage	$
Home Phone	$
Cell Phone	$
TV/ Internet	$
TOTAL	

TRANSPORTATION	
Car Payment	$
Insurance	$
Maintenance	$
Fuel	$
	$
	$
TOTAL	

PERSONAL	
Gym	$
Hair/ Grooming	$
Clothes/ Shoes	$
Vacation	$
Veterinarian	$
TOTAL	

LOANS/DEBT	
Student	$
Personal	$
Credit Cards	$
	$
	$
TOTAL	

MEDICAL	
Doctor	$
Dentist	$
Pharmacy	$
TOTAL	

OTHER	
	$
	$
	$
	$
	$
	$
	$
	$
	$
	$
TOTAL	

INCOME	
Date:	$
Date:	$
Date:	$
Date:	$
TOTAL	

TOTAL INCOME		TOTAL EXPENSES		DIFFERENCE	

Expense Tracker

DATE	DESCRIPTION	CATEGORY	AMOUNT
		TOTAL EXPENSE	

Expense Tracker

DATE	DESCRIPTION	CATEGORY	AMOUNT

TOTAL EXPENSE	

Expense Tracker

DATE	DESCRIPTION	CATEGORY	AMOUNT

TOTAL EXPENSE

Expense Tracker

DATE	DESCRIPTION	CATEGORY	AMOUNT
		TOTAL EXPENSE	

Expense Tracker

DATE	DESCRIPTION	CATEGORY	AMOUNT
		TOTAL EXPENSE	

Savings Summary

DATE	EMERGENCY FUND	SAVINGS	INVESTMENT

TOTAL SAVINGS	

Debt Snowball

List debts smallest to largest. Pay down the smallest debt while paying the minimum payment on all the other debt.

NAME DEBT.	TOTAL BALANCE	MINIMUM PAYMENT	SNOWBALL PAYMENT
TOTAL			

Total Balance - Total Payment = New Balance

Pay off Goals

Amount of months set to pay off smallest debt = _____

Surplus needed each month to reach this goal (smallest debt ÷ number of months) = _____

(Interest not included in calculation)

My mindset "WAS"

My mindset "IS"

My prayer is

Scripture reading

Recovering All

> "The wise have wealth and luxury but the foolish spend whatever they get"
>
> -PROVERBS 21:20

Monthly View

MONTH & YEAR: _____

THIS MONTH'S GOALS

....
....
....
....

WEEKLY GOALS

....
....
....
....

DAILY GOALS

....
....
....
....

SUN	MON	TUE	WED	THU	FRI	SAT

Monthly Budget

HOME	
Mortgage/ Rent	$
Home Insurance	$
Maintenance	$
TOTAL	

CHILDREN	
Child Care	$
Sports	$
	$
TOTAL	

UTILITIES	
Electricity	$
Water/ Sewer	$
Garbage	$
Home Phone	$
Cell Phone	$
TV/ Internet	$
TOTAL	

TRANSPORTATION	
Car Payment	$
Insurance	$
Maintenance	$
Fuel	$
	$
	$
TOTAL	

PERSONAL	
Gym	$
Hair/ Grooming	$
Clothes/ Shoes	$
Vacation	$
Veterinarian	$
TOTAL	

LOANS/DEBT	
Student	$
Personal	$
Credit Cards	$
	$
	$
TOTAL	

MEDICAL	
Doctor	$
Dentist	$
Pharmacy	$
TOTAL	

OTHER	
	$
	$
	$
	$
	$
	$
	$
	$
	$
TOTAL	

INCOME	
Date:	$
Date:	$
Date:	$
Date:	$
TOTAL	

TOTAL INCOME	TOTAL EXPENSES	DIFFERENCE

Expense Tracker

DATE	DESCRIPTION	CATEGORY	AMOUNT
		TOTAL EXPENSE	

Expense Tracker

DATE	DESCRIPTION	CATEGORY	AMOUNT
		TOTAL EXPENSE	

Expense Tracker

DATE	DESCRIPTION	CATEGORY	AMOUNT
		TOTAL EXPENSE	

Expense Tracker

DATE	DESCRIPTION	CATEGORY	AMOUNT
		TOTAL EXPENSE	

Expense Tracker

DATE	DESCRIPTION	CATEGORY	AMOUNT
		TOTAL EXPENSE	

Savings Summary

DATE	EMERGENCY FUND	SAVINGS	INVESTMENT

| TOTAL SAVINGS | |

Debt Snowball

List debts smallest to largest. Pay down the smallest debt while paying the minimum payment on all the other debt.

NAME DEBT.	TOTAL BALANCE	MINIMUM PAYMENT	SNOWBALL PAYMENT
TOTAL			

Total Balance - Total Payment = New Balance

Pay off Goals

Amount of months set to pay off smallest debt = _____

Surplus needed each month to reach this goal (smallest debt ÷ number of months) = _____

(Interest not included in calculation)

Am I working hard by cutting some luxuries and conveniences for a period of time to reach my debt payoff and savings goals?

Am I spending a lot less or a little less money each month? Explain

What disciplines have I developed?

Am I spending time daily with God and developing our relationship? Explain

My prayer is

Scripture reading

Believing Is Achieving

> "Owe nothing to anyone except for your obligation to love one another"
>
> -ROMANS 13:8

Monthly View

MONTH & YEAR: _____

THIS MONTH'S GOALS

WEEKLY GOALS

DAILY GOALS

SUN	MON	TUE	WED	THU	FRI	SAT

Monthly Budget

HOME	
Mortgage/ Rent	$
Home Insurance	$
Maintenance	$
TOTAL	

CHILDREN	
Child Care	$
Sports	$
	$
TOTAL	

UTILITIES	
Electricity	$
Water/ Sewer	$
Garbage	$
Home Phone	$
Cell Phone	$
TV/ Internet	$
TOTAL	

TRANSPORTATION	
Car Payment	$
Insurance	$
Maintenance	$
Fuel	$
	$
	$
TOTAL	

PERSONAL	
Gym	$
Hair/ Grooming	$
Clothes/ Shoes	$
Vacation	$
Veterinarian	$
TOTAL	

LOANS/DEBT	
Student	$
Personal	$
Credit Cards	$
	$
	$
TOTAL	

MEDICAL	
Doctor	$
Dentist	$
Pharmacy	$
TOTAL	

OTHER	
	$
	$
	$
	$
	$
	$
	$
	$
	$
TOTAL	

INCOME	
Date:	$
Date:	$
Date:	$
Date:	$
TOTAL	

TOTAL INCOME	TOTAL EXPENSES	DIFFERENCE

Expense Tracker

DATE	DESCRIPTION	CATEGORY	AMOUNT

| | | TOTAL EXPENSE | |

Expense Tracker

DATE	DESCRIPTION	CATEGORY	AMOUNT

TOTAL EXPENSE

Expense Tracker

DATE	DESCRIPTION	CATEGORY	AMOUNT
		TOTAL EXPENSE	

Expense Tracker

DATE	DESCRIPTION	CATEGORY	AMOUNT
		TOTAL EXPENSE	

Expense Tracker

DATE	DESCRIPTION	CATEGORY	AMOUNT
		TOTAL EXPENSE	

Savings Summary

DATE	EMERGENCY FUND	SAVINGS	INVESTMENT

TOTAL SAVINGS	

Debt Snowball

List debts smallest to largest. Pay down the smallest debt while paying the minimum payment on all the other debt.

NAME DEBT.	TOTAL BALANCE	MINIMUM PAYMENT	SNOWBALL PAYMENT
TOTAL			

Total Balance - Total Payment = New Balance

Pay off Goals

Amount of months set to pay off smallest debt = _____

Surplus needed each month to reach this goal (smallest debt ÷ number of months) = _____
(Interest not included in calculation)

How will being debt free impact my life?

Have I paid down my debt snowball this month?

Did I achieve last month's goal? Why or why not?

My prayer is

Scripture reading

The New Me

> "You will be blessed when you come in and blessed when you go out"
>
> -DEUTERONOMY 28:6

Monthly View

MONTH & YEAR: _____

THIS MONTH'S GOALS

_____
_____
_____
_____
_____

WEEKLY GOALS

_____
_____
_____
_____
_____

DAILY GOALS

_____
_____
_____
_____
_____

SUN	MON	TUE	WED	THU	FRI	SAT

Monthly Budget

HOME	
Mortgage/ Rent	$
Home Insurance	$
Maintenance	$
TOTAL	

UTILITIES	
Electricity	$
Water/ Sewer	$
Garbage	$
Home Phone	$
Cell Phone	$
TV/ Internet	$
TOTAL	

PERSONAL	
Gym	$
Hair/ Grooming	$
Clothes/ Shoes	$
Vacation	$
Veterinarian	$
TOTAL	

MEDICAL	
Doctor	$
Dentist	$
Pharmacy	$
TOTAL	

INCOME	
Date:	$
Date:	$
Date:	$
Date:	$
TOTAL	

CHILDREN	
Child Care	$
Sports	$
	$
TOTAL	

TRANSPORTATION	
Car Payment	$
Insurance	$
Maintenance	$
Fuel	$
	$
	$
TOTAL	

LOANS/DEBT	
Student	$
Personal	$
Credit Cards	$
	$
	$
TOTAL	

OTHER	
	$
	$
	$
	$
	$
	$
	$
	$
	$
TOTAL	

TOTAL INCOME   TOTAL EXPENSES   DIFFERENCE

Expense Tracker

DATE	DESCRIPTION	CATEGORY	AMOUNT
		TOTAL EXPENSE	

Expense Tracker

DATE	DESCRIPTION	CATEGORY	AMOUNT
		TOTAL EXPENSE	

Expense Tracker

DATE	DESCRIPTION	CATEGORY	AMOUNT
		TOTAL EXPENSE	

Expense Tracker

DATE	DESCRIPTION	CATEGORY	AMOUNT
		TOTAL EXPENSE	

Expense Tracker

DATE	DESCRIPTION	CATEGORY	AMOUNT

TOTAL EXPENSE

Savings Summary

DATE	EMERGENCY FUND	SAVINGS	INVESTMENT

TOTAL SAVINGS

Debt Snowball

List debts smallest to largest. Pay down the smallest debt while paying the minimum payment on all the other debt.

NAME DEBT.	TOTAL BALANCE	MINIMUM PAYMENT	SNOWBALL PAYMENT
TOTAL			

Total Balance - Total Payment = New Balance

Pay off Goals

Amount of months set to pay off smallest debt = _____

Surplus needed each month to reach this goal (smallest debt ÷ number of months) = _____
(Interest not included in calculation)

How are my spending habits?

What expenses will I cut out this month?

How will I achieve this?

My prayer is

Scripture reading

In The Abundance

"Bring tithe into my storehouse, if you do, says the lord I will open up the windows of heaven. I will pour you out a blessing you won't have room to receive"

-MALACHI 3:9-10

Monthly View

MONTH & YEAR: _____

THIS MONTH'S GOALS

....
....
....
....
....

WEEKLY GOALS

....
....
....
....
....

DAILY GOALS

....
....
....
....
....

SUN	MON	TUE	WED	THU	FRI	SAT

Monthly Budget

HOME	
Mortgage/ Rent	$
Home Insurance	$
Maintenance	$
TOTAL	

CHILDREN	
Child Care	$
Sports	$
	$
TOTAL	

UTILITIES	
Electricity	$
Water/ Sewer	$
Garbage	$
Home Phone	$
Cell Phone	$
TV/ Internet	$
TOTAL	

TRANSPORTATION	
Car Payment	$
Insurance	$
Maintenance	$
Fuel	$
	$
	$
TOTAL	

PERSONAL	
Gym	$
Hair/ Grooming	$
Clothes/ Shoes	$
Vacation	$
Veterinarian	$
TOTAL	

LOANS/DEBT	
Student	$
Personal	$
Credit Cards	$
	$
	$
TOTAL	

MEDICAL	
Doctor	$
Dentist	$
Pharmacy	$
TOTAL	

OTHER	
	$
	$
	$
	$
	$
	$
	$
	$
	$
	$
TOTAL	

INCOME	
Date:	$
Date:	$
Date:	$
Date:	$
TOTAL	

TOTAL INCOME		TOTAL EXPENSES		DIFFERENCE	

Expense Tracker

DATE	DESCRIPTION	CATEGORY	AMOUNT
		TOTAL EXPENSE	

Expense Tracker

DATE	DESCRIPTION	CATEGORY	AMOUNT
		TOTAL EXPENSE	

Expense Tracker

DATE	DESCRIPTION	CATEGORY	AMOUNT
		TOTAL EXPENSE	

Expense Tracker

DATE	DESCRIPTION	CATEGORY	AMOUNT
		TOTAL EXPENSE	

Expense Tracker

DATE	DESCRIPTION	CATEGORY	AMOUNT

TOTAL EXPENSE

Savings Summary

DATE	EMERGENCY FUND	SAVINGS	INVESTMENT

TOTAL SAVINGS	

Debt Snowball

List debts smallest to largest. Pay down the smallest debt while paying the minimum payment on all the other debt.

NAME DEBT.	TOTAL BALANCE	MINIMUM PAYMENT	SNOWBALL PAYMENT
TOTAL			

Total Balance - Total Payment = New Balance

Pay off Goals

Amount of months set to pay off smallest debt = _____

plus needed each month to reach this goal (smallest debt ÷ number of months) = _____
(Interest not included in calculation)

Financial Plans

My financial plans are

What is my purpose for striving to achieve these plans

My prayer is

Scripture reading

Undeniable

"But blessed are those who trust in the Lord and have made the Lord their hope and confidence. They are like the trees planted by the rivers of water their deeply rooted to reach the water. These trees are not bothered by long months of drought. They never stop producing fruit"

-ROMANS 13:8

Monthly View

MONTH & YEAR: _____

THIS MONTH'S GOALS

_____
_____
_____
_____

WEEKLY GOALS

_____
_____
_____
_____

DAILY GOALS

_____
_____
_____
_____

SUN	MON	TUE	WED	THU	FRI	SAT

Monthly Budget

HOME	
Mortgage/ Rent	$
Home Insurance	$
Maintenance	$
TOTAL	

CHILDREN	
Child Care	$
Sports	$
	$
TOTAL	

UTILITIES	
Electricity	$
Water/ Sewer	$
Garbage	$
Home Phone	$
Cell Phone	$
TV/ Internet	$
TOTAL	

TRANSPORTATION	
Car Payment	$
Insurance	$
Maintenance	$
Fuel	$
	$
	$
TOTAL	

PERSONAL	
Gym	$
Hair/ Grooming	$
Clothes/ Shoes	$
Vacation	$
Veterinarian	$
TOTAL	

LOANS/DEBT	
Student	$
Personal	$
Credit Cards	$
	$
	$
TOTAL	

MEDICAL	
Doctor	$
Dentist	$
Pharmacy	$
TOTAL	

OTHER	
	$
	$
	$
	$
	$
	$
	$
	$
	$
TOTAL	

INCOME	
Date:	$
Date:	$
Date:	$
Date:	$
TOTAL	

TOTAL INCOME		TOTAL EXPENSES		DIFFERENCE	

Expense Tracker

DATE	DESCRIPTION	CATEGORY	AMOUNT
		TOTAL EXPENSE	

Expense Tracker

DATE	DESCRIPTION	CATEGORY	AMOUNT
		TOTAL EXPENSE	

Expense Tracker

DATE	DESCRIPTION	CATEGORY	AMOUNT
		TOTAL EXPENSE	

Expense Tracker

DATE	DESCRIPTION	CATEGORY	AMOUNT
		TOTAL EXPENSE	

Expense Tracker

DATE	DESCRIPTION	CATEGORY	AMOUNT
		TOTAL EXPENSE	

Savings Summary

DATE	EMERGENCY FUND	SAVINGS	INVESTMENT

TOTAL SAVINGS	

Debt Snowball

List debts smallest to largest. Pay down the smallest debt while paying the minimum payment on all the other debt.

NAME DEBT.	TOTAL BALANCE	MINIMUM PAYMENT	SNOWBALL PAYMENT
TOTAL			

Total Balance - Total Payment = New Balance

Pay off Goals

Amount of months set to pay off smallest debt = _____

Surplus needed each month to reach this goal (smallest debt ÷ number of months) = _____
(Interest not included in calculation)

What kind of results am I seeing from the changes that I have implemented

Am I putting the neccessary work in to reach my goals as quickly as possible? Why or why not?

My prayer is

Scripture reading

Change

> "And have put on a new self, which is being renewed in knowledge after the image of its creator"
>
> -COLOSSIANS 3:10

Monthly View

MONTH & YEAR: _____

THIS MONTH'S GOALS

_____
_____
_____
_____

WEEKLY GOALS

_____
_____
_____
_____

DAILY GOALS

_____
_____
_____

SUN	MON	TUE	WED	THU	FRI	SAT

Monthly Budget

HOME	
Mortgage/ Rent	$
Home Insurance	$
Maintenance	$
TOTAL	

CHILDREN	
Child Care	$
Sports	$
	$
TOTAL	

UTILITIES	
Electricity	$
Water/ Sewer	$
Garbage	$
Home Phone	$
Cell Phone	$
TV/ Internet	$
TOTAL	

TRANSPORTATION	
Car Payment	$
Insurance	$
Maintenance	$
Fuel	$
	$
	$
TOTAL	

PERSONAL	
Gym	$
Hair/ Grooming	$
Clothes/ Shoes	$
Vacation	$
Veterinarian	$
TOTAL	

LOANS/DEBT	
Student	$
Personal	$
Credit Cards	$
	$
	$
TOTAL	

MEDICAL	
Doctor	$
Dentist	$
Pharmacy	$
TOTAL	

OTHER	
	$
	$
	$
	$
	$
	$
	$
	$
	$
TOTAL	

INCOME	
Date:	$
Date:	$
Date:	$
Date:	$
TOTAL	

TOTAL INCOME		TOTAL EXPENSES		DIFFERENCE	

Expense Tracker

DATE	DESCRIPTION	CATEGORY	AMOUNT
			TOTAL EXPENSE

Expense Tracker

DATE	DESCRIPTION	CATEGORY	AMOUNT
		TOTAL EXPENSE	

Expense Tracker

DATE	DESCRIPTION	CATEGORY	AMOUNT
		TOTAL EXPENSE	

Expense Tracker

DATE	DESCRIPTION	CATEGORY	AMOUNT
		TOTAL EXPENSE	

Expense Tracker

DATE	DESCRIPTION	CATEGORY	AMOUNT

TOTAL EXPENSE	

Savings Summary

DATE	EMERGENCY FUND	SAVINGS	INVESTMENT

TOTAL SAVINGS

Debt Snowball

List debts smallest to largest. Pay down the smallest debt while paying the minimum payment on all the other debt.

NAME DEBT.	TOTAL BALANCE	MINIMUM PAYMENT	SNOWBALL PAYMENT
TOTAL			

Total Balance - Total Payment = New Balance

_____

Pay off Goals

Amount of months set to pay off smallest debt = _____

plus needed each month to reach this goal (smallest debt ÷ number of months) = _____
(Interest not included in calculation)

What have I learned about myself over the past 12 months?

What did I accomplish on this journey?

My prayer is

Scripture reading

End Of The Year Summary

MONTH	INCOME	SAVINGS	Debt-1 amount paid	Debt-2 amount paid	Debt-3 amount paid	Debt-4 amount paid
TOTAL						

Debt Remaining Balance

DEBT1	DEBT2	DEBT3	DEBT4

Made in United States
Troutdale, OR
09/27/2023

13230367R00092